EDDIE THOMPSON

POETRY
Free Range

&

More verses about life

With drawings by Peter Osborne

EDDIE THOMPSON

POETRY
Free Range

More verses about life

With drawings by Peter Osborne

MEREO
Cirencester

Mereo Books

1A The Wool Market Dyer Street Cirencester Gloucestershire GL7 2PR

An imprint of Memoirs Publishing www.mereobooks.com

Poetry Free Range: 978-1-86151-727-2

First published in Great Britain in 2016
by Mereo Books, an imprint of Memoirs Publishing

Copyright ©2016

Eddie Thompson has asserted his Right under the Copyright Designs and Patents Act 1988 to be identified as the author of this work.

This book is a work of fiction and except in the case of historical fact any resemblance to actual persons living or dead is purely coincidental.

A CIP catalogue record for this book is available from the British Library.

This book is sold subject to the condition that it shall not by way of trade or otherwise be lent, resold, hired out or otherwise circulated without the publisher's prior consent in any form of binding or cover, other than that in which it is published and without a similar condition, including this condition being imposed on the subsequent purchaser.

The address for Memoirs Publishing Group Limited can be found at
www.memoirspublishing.com

The Memoirs Publishing Group Ltd Reg. No. 7834348

The Memoirs Publishing Group supports both The Forest Stewardship Council® (FSC®) and the PEFC® leading international forest-certification organisations. Our books carrying both the FSC label and the PEFC® and are printed on FSC®-certified paper. FSC® is the only forest-certification scheme supported by the leading environmental organisations including Greenpeace. Our paper procurement policy can be found at
www.memoirspublishing.com/environment

Typeset in 9/15pt Bembo
by Wiltshire Associates Publisher Services Ltd. Printed and bound in Great Britain by
Printondemand-Worldwide, Peterborough PE2 6XD

ABOUT THE AUTHOR

Eddie Thompson is an expatriate Manxman who settled in Milton Keynes with his Welsh wife Enid and daughters Kirsty and Gill in 1981. Encouraged by seeing his first book of verses, Poetry Lite, published, Eddie has unearthed more of his work, again enhanced by Peter Osborne's drawings, for this second collection. He writes:

> *The plan was to list events and thoughts*
> *Record them all in rhyme*
> *The problem is, there's not a lot of either*
> *And now I'm running out of time.*

Peter Osborne writes: "I love to put aside my oils and palette and join my friend Eddie Thompson, the wordsmith, poet and sideswiper, and add a few visuals to his verbals."

Also by Eddie Thompson
Poetry Lite

To Enid, Kirsty and Gill

The quality of these verses
Is liable to change;
The writer's mind is unconfined,
It operates free range.

INTRODUCTION

This is a selection
From a collection
Of poetry, so-called,
An apology
Of an anthology;
Prepare to be appalled.

CONTENTS

Short ones

Limericks

Six-liners

Long ones

Longer ones

SHORT ONES

In case you wonder
It's not poems by the yard,
It's five lines or under
And limericks are barred.

Evolution
People
Remote Control
Self-awareness
Fur Trade
Twinkle Twinkle
OK, I'm irrational
Methodism
Ithyphallic
Premier Division
The MML
Cocoa
Cocoa (2)
Hope springs eternal
The selection process
Thatcherism and Wales
A worker's dwelling
Place names
Hope springs eternal (2)
Hoping for a resurrection

EVOLUTION

What lies ahead re natural selection?
What next, on our evolutionary ladder?
Possibly extra-sensory perception,
Personally I'd prefer a bigger bladder.

PEOPLE

There are some who fill up our tanks with their gasoline
And others who are clearly the grit in life's Vaseline.*

*'The grit in life's Vaseline' – a phrase from the song 'Leopold Allcocks', by Jake Thackray.

REMOTE CONTROL

No one enters our life by chance,
Some come to test but most to enhance,
Nothing is as it seems on the surface,
Everyone enter our lives for a purpose.

SELF-AWARENESS

Beware the ills of self-inflation
And its popular partner self-adulation
Keep in mind self-preservation,
As in time they will lead to self-denigration
And that terrible punishment, self-condemnation.

FUR TRADE

What? Wipe my bum with the cat!
On my honour, I couldn't do that,
What an unhygienic habit,
Besides, I always use the rabbit.

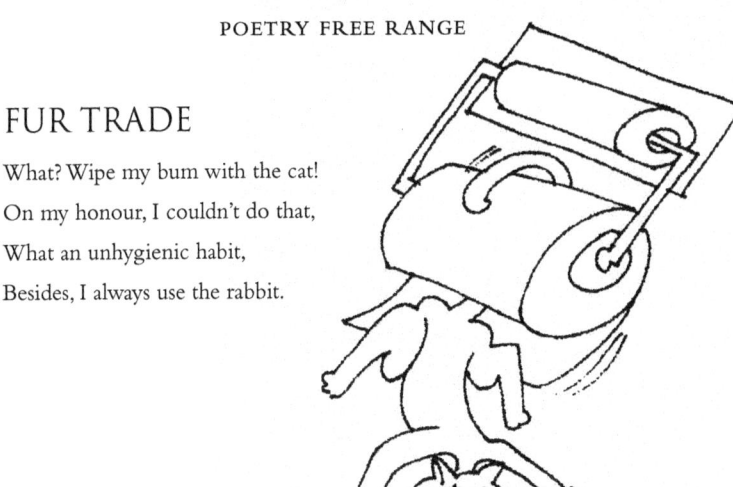

TWINKLE TWINKLE...

To all ophthalmic surgeons I offer this little wrinkle,
Yes, remove the cataract, but leave in place the twinkle.

OK, I'M IRRATIONAL

I stand accused of being irrational,
To me that isn't a flaw
For show me a rational person,
And I'll show you a crashing bore.

METHODISM

The Sabbath was strictly a no-fun day,
That was the rule and boy did they employ it.
Sex was allowed in certain cases,
Providing you didn't enjoy it.

ITHYPHALLIC

Ithyphallic?
It came up on a course
of primitive religion.
(No pun intended).

PREMIER DIVISION

Faith v Reason
Apostolicam Ecclesiam 1, Hamilton Academical 1

THE MML

For riveting reading and prose to adore,
Try the Annual Manual of Military Law.

COCOA

It's cocoa for vivid dreams,
Tell your friends it's more than it seems,
Spread the word throughout the land,
Stock up now, before it's banned.

COCOA (2)

"Repent, the end of the world is nigh",
Relent, drink cocoa, go out on a high.

HOPE SPRINGS ETERNAL

My my, Edward dear, what is this I feel?
Are you glad to see me? Have I such appeal?
Yes and yes again, and I love this warm embrace,
But what you feel my dearest, is my glasses case.

THE SELECTION PROCESS

She may be a ravishing beauty, a paragon, a jewel
But does she understand the LBW rule?

THATCHERISM AND WALES

Thatcherism, that Tory totem,
Is as welcome in Wales
As a boil on the scrotum.

A WORKER'S DWELLING

A two-up two-down council house at seven and six a week
In 1937, to us, was a des res, so to speak
To keep us in our place, and this is worth the telling,
It was described upon the rent card, as "A Worker's Dwelling".

PLACE NAMES

Newport Pagnell, Shepton Mallet, Corfe Mullen,
These place names have a ring about them,
They sort of make you want to shout them,
I'm sure that they are interesting, anything but dull,
But can they be as interesting as single-syllabled Hull?

HOPE SPRINGS ETERNAL (2)

"What!" said Enid, "Hot Sex?"
"No," said Edward, 'Hut Six".

HOPING FOR A RESURRECTION

Even to his doctor he just will not mention,
The fact that his soldier no longer stands to attention.

LIMERICKS

Limericks are not very highly regarded,
Their writers are seen as slightly retarded
With smut they're synonymous,
And their writers anonymous,
If they weren't they'd be booked and red-carded.

Why do I feel so uneasy?

Reunions

Milton Keynes

A limerick in traditional vein

Enhancement

The other elixir of life (2)

Ten am

The finest upright organ

Victorious

GFH

WHY DO I FEEL SO UNEASY?

Why do I feel so uneasy?
What is it that makes me so queasy?
It's because our society
Has gained notoriety
By becoming increasingly sleazy.

REUNIONS

What fun, what joy, what utter bliss,
To meet again and reminisce,
To laugh and sigh
About days gone by,
To join old comrades on the piss.

MILTON KEYNES

We in MK ask you all to relent
From making sick jokes with malicious intent
'Bout the cows in our field
Who, instead of milk, yield
Three of gravel, one of sand, and one of cement.

A LIMERICK IN TRADITIONAL VEIN

An adventurous young couple from Rhyl,
Searched for the ultimate thrill,
They tried sex gay and straight
And found bondage was great,
And being tied up at weekends just brill.

ENHANCEMENT

Slapping on your make-up, surface flaws suppressing,
Enhancing Mother Nature to keep your suitors guessing
It brings to mind agricultural knowledge,
A tip that's taught in agricultural college:
"Poor sub-soil needs a lot of top dressing."

THE OTHER ELIXIR OF LIFE 2

It's enough to hatch hysteria,
This supposedly superior
(Do my eyes deceive?
Am I meant to believe?)
Guinness from Nigeria?

TEN AM

Please don't call before ten
As I'm half asleep until then
So unless it's a must,
Or you're driven by lust,
Please do not call before ten.

THE FINEST UPRIGHT ORGAN

At the home of the Reverend Pritchard-Pugh
On Wednesdays and Saturdays visitors can view
The finest upright organ
In the whole of Mid-Glamorgan
It is impressive, be prepared to queue.

VICTORIOUS

Gloria! Gloria! and yet again, Gloria!
Can't you just feel our collective euphoria?
And it's all because
Of our wonder from Oz,
The lovely, delightful, distinguished Victoria.★

GFH

It doesn't get any better than this,
For me it's the ultimate bliss,
To sing in a choir
Handel's Messiah,
George Frederick Handel, your feet I would kiss.

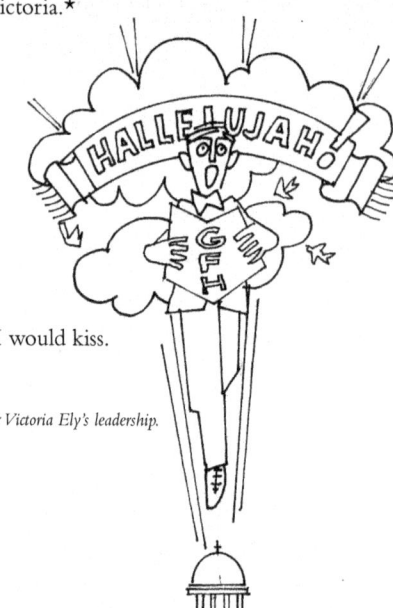

★*Alter MK Chorale's Spring Concert, our first under Victoria Ely's leadership.*

SIX LINERS

Six short lines, this suits my attention span,
And if one bores you, it won't bore you for long
That too is part of the cunning plan,
Some will, of that, without doubt I'm not wrong,
I could prune them still further, but, on second thoughts,
I'll leave them as they are, with their blemishes and warts.

Ageing
The luxury of time
Phobias
Ageing (2)
Ageing (3)
Black puddings for breakfast
Impure Thoughts
"Defensive Mechanism"
Flags and drums
Elementary, my dear Watson
A lost soul
Enlightenment
February 14th
Family trees
The Groom of the Stool
Gliese 581c
Re the women's new blouses
GUH or Wendy Cope?
Women and rhythm
Griff
Me
A Lothario pierced
Judgement Day
Jerry Gill
Guardians of the airways
Reincarnation
Poetry and poets
John and Emily
Catherine of Aragon
Doris and Maurice
Poetry
It's that collared dove again
Cyril the Squirrel v the Thieving Magpie
Porridge and prunes
Senokot, for a moving experience
I wonder
The Meaning of Life
Sing me The Messiah
Army speak
Something profound
Reginald the Second
The Duckworth Lewis method
George Fox
Overheard in a bookshop
Mr Rodriguez
Things esoteric
Manx knobs
Hug me
`Normality'?
Guess Who?

AGEING

The odd 'senior moment' was once appealing,
But now they're the norm, I can't help feeling
That the dreaded abyss is rapidly nearing
The startling cascade I'm definitely hearing.
"Oh come on, admit it, you just like to suffer,
Come on, own up, you're a silly old duffer."

THE LUXURY OF TIME

"What means this life if full of care,
We have no time to stand and stare?"★
We have no time to stand and stare, sadly that's a fact
Some of us have tried it, sadly they were sacked.
And as for your question, framed well in rhyme,
Sadly we can't help you, we haven't got the time.

★*From "Leisure", by William Henry Davies.*

PHOBIAS

We all have an Achilles' heel,
A weakness that can put us on an uneven keel,
The imagined ridicule, the mocking, the sneers,
Prevent us from facing up to our fears,
I have my own boil to lance,
The illogical fear of getting up to dance.

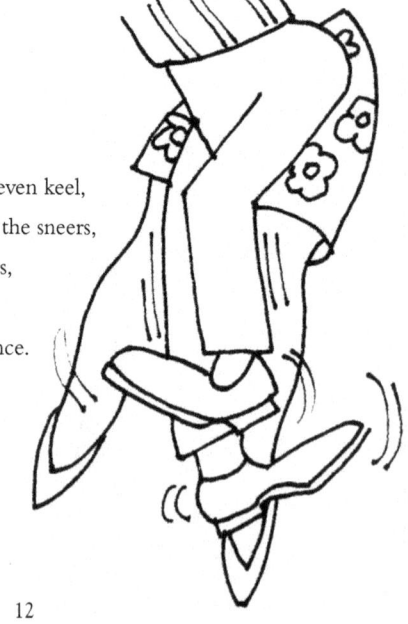

AGEING (2)

I just don't care what you say, it *is* depressing knowing
That hair, teeth and eyesight
Though not gone, are going.
Do not be distressed my son, though 'tis old you're growing,
Be grateful this and every day,
That your embers are still glowing.

AGEING (3)

It must be my age,
I have read it's so, at this late stage
But nothing can surprise me, let alone excite me
It's time to recognize it, nothing can ignite me.
But really, is this me, emotionless, devoid of passion?
Yes, it is, apparently, I have used up my ration.

*After realizing that whilst football fans around me were in a frenzy of elation or anger, I was thinking about tomorrow's breakfast.

BLACK PUDDINGS FOR BREAKFAST

Black puddings for breakfast,
It's hedonistic debauchery,
Culinary sorcery
So put the cornflakes back in the packet,
Put yourself in a different bracket,
It's black puddings for breakfast.

IMPURE THOUGHTS

Why confess our "impure thoughts"?
Why liken them to genital warts?
They're perfectly natural, completely untaught,
So why is the church so uptight, so fraught?
They're just fantasies that come to naught,
They're wishful thinking – an in-house sport.

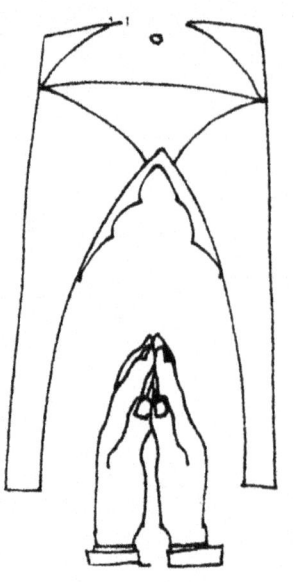

"DEFENSIVE PESSIMISM"

Defensive pessimism, add it to the list,
Write it on my label – 'He is a pessimist".
Positive thinking is now overrated,
It's flogged to death and seemingly outdated.
So for those of us with a half empty cup,
It's cool! Pessimism is on the way up.

FLAGS AND DRUMS

Flags and drums get adrenalin flowing, in some
For others, they act as a warning of something dreadful to come
They serve as a rallying call, to conquer or defend
Either way, there'll be death, on that you can depend.
But people will never stop marching behind the flag and the drum
'Twas ever thus and ever will be, 'till thy kingdom come.

ELEMENTARY, MY DEAR WATSON

I say Watson, what do we have here?
Teeth marks on the toilet door knob, deep and crystal clear,
Whatever can it mean? said Watson, what can you deduce?
It's such a strange phenomenon, is it any use?
Elementary, shouted Holmes, after a moment's contemplation
Our suspect clearly suffers from severe constipation.

A LOST SOUL

Oh shaman, shaman, help me please,
I fear I've lost my soul,
Go flying high above the trees,
Beat your drum and shin your pole,
I beg you, down upon my knees,
Find it – make me whole.

ENLIGHTENMENT

A sober, celibate Calvinist
Being curious, kept a tryst
With the barmaid at the Old Swan Inn
And spent the night in blissful sin.
On realizing what he has missed,
He spends his Sundays getting pissed.

FEBRUARY 14TH

Who do I think of by day and by night?
Who makes me feel as high as a kite?
Who do I place above all the rest?
Who do I think is simply the best?
Don't think me pathetic,
It's Wigan Athletic.

FAMILY TREES

So this is what we're destined to be,
A name, on a branch, on a family tree
A name and two dates after 'b' and a 'd',
A life in two lines, with luck maybe three,
And in a shoe box, under a bed,
An unknown, on a photograph, long since dead.

THE GROOM OF THE STOOL

To be 'Groom of the Stool', an old royal appointment,

One needed a nose for promotion

A long handled brush and a huge jar of ointment,

The last to lube the King's motion,

And though close to the throne, the great and the grand,

There was a reluctance to shake the Groom's hand.

The Groom of the Stool was a position created by Henry VIII; his function was to attend to Henry's every lavatorial need.

GLIESE 581C

You're never, ever, far from my thoughts,

You potentially promising planet of sorts

To your alluring attractions excitement I own,

Orbiting there in your 'Goldilocks zone'.

Are you our salvation, to which we can flee?

Oh firmament of the cosmos, Five eight one c.

RE THE WOMEN'S NEW BLOUSES

Re the women's new blouses in the Chorale
I have to say bluntly, they've lowered morale.
I think of the days when they chose what they wore
White see-through blouses, with cleavage galore.
The men now agree that the next ones they get,
Will be tight-fitting T-shirts, worn preferably wet.

GMH OR WENDY COPE?

Verse by Gerard Manley Hopkins totally frustrates me,
Its bottomless cryptic meaning totally escapes me
The message it conveys is beyond my understanding,
It's opaque to me, obscure, intellectually demanding.
To decipher and digest it I haven't got a hope,
So for poetry that lifts me, I shall stay with Wendy Cope.

WOMEN AND RHYTHM

To rhythm women are more attuned,
In rhythm women are soon cocooned
Watch them when there's rhythm about,
They shimmy and shake, twist and shout
Why are we men so stiff, so staid?
Admit it men, we dance in their shade.

GRIFF

Our good friend Griff will study a menu for ages,
When the meals at last arrive, you can bet your next week's wages
"I should have ordered that", he'll say, admiring another's choice,
With more than a hint of regret in his Welsh tenor voice
To commemorate this indecision, his family have debated
And they'll put upon his headstone: 'I should have been cremated'.

ME

Neither alcoholic
Nor apostolic
Pessimism
Is my ism,
My other folly?
I'm melancholy.

A LOTHARIO PIERCED

"I fell in love, hook line and scrotum." Who said that and when?
It's a quote of note and your starter for ten.
It was Errol Flynn, in the late nineteen-forties,
Describing one of his sexual sorties
But Pat Wymore was no routine catch,
Errol Flynn had met his match.

JUDGEMENT DAY

Every day is Judgement Day, with self as defendant and judge,
Evidence is laid before me, evidence I cannot fudge
Mitigating circumstances? There's not a one in sight,
Nevertheless I'm standing tall, well aware of my plight
Of course I plead guilty as charged, then I don the Black Cap,
Every day is Judgement Day: it's a self- tormenting trap.

JERRY GILL

Round-faced, rosy-faced Manxman Jerry Gill
'Though dead these many years, in my mind I see him still,
Husband, father, gardener, and always with a smile,
A man to have at your side when going that extra mile,
He knew well the English Channel, that all important seaway,
Being fished out at Dunkirk and thrown back in on D-Day.

GUARDIANS OF THE AIRWAYS

They may look a mess
And they get a bad press
But they're valuable sentries,
Guarding vulnerable entries.
Regard them as bouncers, filtering foes,
Those hairs in your ears, and those in your nose.

REINCARNATION

Do our souls lie fallow between each existence?
Do we have a choice, can we show resistance?
By whom, what and why are we reincarnated?
Is each new beginning performance-related?
Is it the Law of Retribution, what one sows one must reap?
If it is I'm in the muck, and in it pretty deep.

POETRY AND POETS

It's the human condition that true poetry explores,
Not the easily understood, versified prose
It's an emotional awareness of our personal flaws,
An expression of self, our cares and our woes,
But there is a worrying warning to those that have the flair:
"A good percentage of poets need professional care."

After visiting poetrymagic.co.uk

JOHN AND EMILY

Emily, Yorkshire born and bred,
John of Essex, wisely wed,
Her family wailed in disbelief,
Thinking she would come to grief,
"Comes the crunch, we'll have to drug 'er,
She's not going to marry a southern bugger."

CATHERINE OF ARAGON

Of virtue a paragon
Catherine of Aragon
How sad she had to marry
Arthur's brother Harry,
The first 'Defender of the Faith',
That sleazeball Henry, Henry the Eighth.

DORIS AND MAURICE

A collared dove, let's call her Doris
And her chosen love, let's call him Maurice
Are building their nest, against our wish,
Between the wall and our TV dish.
We won't object to their billing and cooing,
Unless it affects our TV viewing.

POETRY

What's the point of poetry? Primarily, what's it for?
Except to those who write it, is it all a crashing bore?
What's the purpose behind it, why do we spend so much time
Finding fitting phrases that marry up message and rhyme?
Is it to gather together feelings that float in your head
Then put them down in words, that would otherwise never be said?

IT'S THAT COLLARED DOVE AGAIN

I cannot love
that collared dove
His call is so peculiar
His boring song
Goes on and on,
Wait - he's stopped. Hallelujah!

CYRIL THE SQUIRREL V. THE THIEVING MAGPIE

Cyril the squirrel buried a nut
And forgot straightway where it was put
A thieving magpie spied the scene,
And plotted a theft, despicably mean
He simply waited till the squirrel had gone,
Cyril nil, magpie one.

PORRIDGE AND PRUNES

Is your waste disposal system dormant?
You can rid yourself of toil and torment
Just open your fridge and have a good forage
For a packet of prunes with a bowl full of porridge
And in ten minutes flat your block will be blown,
Be sure you're on a toilet, preferably your own.

SENOKOT, FOR A MOVING EXPERIENCE

I'm never too far from a toilet
After my Senokot overdose
For me, it's a lesson well learnt,
To a laxative, never get over-close,
It's much more than a chronic irritation,
It's a primitive form of colonic irrigation.

I WONDER

I wonder, was a missionary
A venerated visionary?
Priest and prototype physician,
Reciting the Creed
As he sowed his seed,
In the missionary position?

THE MEANING OF LIFE

"What's the mysterious meaning of life?"
I recently asked my beloved wife
'Where do we fit in the cosmos, dear?
What's the point of us being here?
Tell me dear heart, be my guide."
"To shop, my beloved, to shop," she replied.

SING ME THE MESSIAH

Sing it loud and sing it well, sing me The Messiah
I'll try to sing along as I'm rolled into my pyre
Nothing bland, you understand, nothing dull or dire
Something that I love to hear, sing me The Messiah.
My sentence has been passed, a millennium in mire
So please, one last request, sing me The Messiah.

ARMY SPEAK

The army's use of language is an art form quite unique
I call it 'catalogue-descriptive', a form of army speak
Take, screw, retaining, intermediate firing needle withdrawal lever
What a picture that must conjure in the mind of the receiver
As a classic example, and I believe there's not one finer,
There's that old inventory entry, "Pots, child, chamber, china".

SOMETHING PROFOUND

I wanted to say something profound,
But after much thought came not a sound
Then, out of the blue, to my memory sprang,
The gist of a phrase by R D Laing
Its appeal lies in its utter starkness:
'To live without love is to walk in darkness'.

REGINALD THE SECOND

Manx-Norse Prince Reginald the Second, King of Man to be,
So the ancient annals reckoned, spent three long years at sea
Did this son of a Viking have problems with life ashore?
Was it not to his liking, did he find it all a bore?
How, we may posit, did his sexual urges abate?
Did he have in the closet a very compliant first mate?

THE DUCKWORTH LEWIS METHOD

This Duckworth Lewis method, what's it all about?
Possibly a process for extracting coal?
Or maybe a means of birth control?
Or a new technique in the brewing of stout?
Will it be recorded in the annals of history
As one great unfathomable, universal mystery?

GEORGE FOX

George won't go on coach trips,
"Too many OAPS, too many dodgy hips,
Too many stops for pees."
His point, I admit, I can clearly see,
He is, after all, only eighty-three.

OVERHEARD IN A BOOKSHOP

I heard this said in a Galway bookshop, some twenty years ago
When a man walked up to the counter, and in a voice far from low,
(I can still hear his question, put in bold but dulcet tones)
"Have you anything here," he said, "On the so-called erogenous zones?"
The assistant, completely unfazed, her customer squarely eyed,
As "Science fiction upstairs sir, turn right at the top," she replied.

MR RODRIGUEZ

My Portuguese dentist loves to chat
About world affairs and this and that
But all the wrong syllables he tends to stress
And often his meaning I'm left to guess
Like the time I heard, "Use the Central Line",
When he actually said, "Use Sensodyne".

THINGS ESOTERIC

I'm greatly attracted to things esoteric,
Like clairvoyancy and things atmospheric
I like to see things in an eerie light,
And believe in things that go bump in the night
And prayer, guardians, Celtic mythology,
Reincarnation and even psychology.

MANX KNOBS

Manx Knobs are sweets
That are sucked and enjoyed as treats
On the tin there's a truth,
Though somewhat uncouth,
Worth pointing out to the wife:
"Manx Knobs vary in size – that's life."

HUG ME

Keep calm and hug me,
Don't alarm or bug me
If all the rivers are running dry,
And the end of the world is apparently nigh,
Don't arm or drug me,
Keep calm and hug me.

'NORMALITY'?

On meeting strangers, we are, well, formal,
We follow 'chapel manners' down to the letter
Then we find that they're not 'normal',
Once we get to know them better.
This oft-repeated finding serves to inform
That not being 'normal' is in fact the norm.

GUESS WHO?

A certain female poet, I will not name her here,
Compiles her verse solely on sexual matters
Her style is frank to the point of giving men much to fear
Suffice to say, it leaves men's egos in tatters
In things erotic she must be well versed,
As in steamy scenes, her thoughts seem immersed.

LONG ONES

Seven lines or over but less than a page
Is judged to be 'long' by this primitive gauge.
It's not the best way of bringing together
What could be called 'birds of a feather',
But arranging by length, for all its quirks,
Has speed and simplicity as major perks.
Besides, some forms of poetry are governed by length
And maybe that discipline adds to their strength.

A close encounter
Altos and the fuller figure
Amongst the aged
In a corner of Linford Wood
Brits, an endangered species
Language difficulties
Cecil and Claude
Hugs
Enthusiasm please!
Internal reassurance
Fenella Fudge
The Family Tree
Friends
Consequences
Hans Litten (1903-1938)
The mugger
Hymn number 193 (A & M Revised)
No sex please, we're British
I cannot do the rumba
Something to try at home?
Continuity
The new regime
Thanks but no thanks
To the children of Uganda
Larkrise Village to Candleford Town
A football fan's wish list
Let's hear it for Anchorites
Litter-pickers wanted
Rhythm
Losers
The optimism of the football fan
O'Donovan's oboe
On not being busy
'Oscar'
Fluid recall
Proper poetry
Roberta of Nash
Rosie and Noel's 60th
Urban studies
So, what do I believe?
Social trends
A flash in the park
Stereotyping
The quaver
The match
The mating game
He can do better
Tommy the Tup's last stand
The soloist
To MK's critics
One for the children
We'll meet again
Harmony
Welsh words
Beryl and Bert
"Who is this guy Biggles?"
The corner shop

A CLOSE ENCOUNTER

She came in close, real close,
Well inside my personal space.
I didn't resist, what man would?
She didn't wear make-up, or none that I could see,
Nor perfume,
But her closeness carried that pleasant whiff of woman.
Glancing down, I glimpsed a sliver of cleavage,
A grey day brightened up.
She peered intensely into my eyes,
Then stepped back,
Leaving my space as abruptly as she had entered it,
And spoke, quietly, confidently,
Breaking the spell, as she asked:
"What line can you read now?"

ALTOS AND THE FULLER FIGURE

To Richard Morrison, choral perfection
Is reached through big bosoms in the alto section
He laments the loss of the Mother Earth figure,
And remembers 'altos when their busts were bigger.
He writes in despair and is obviously grieving
At the absence of bosoms ample and heaving.
Well in Milton Keynes, I can tell him for sure,
That 'altos here his despair would cure
Here they sing for all their worth,
With bosoms of enormous girth
With bosoms so big that to allay their fears,
Their bras are designed by engineers.

After reading "Whatever happened to that bosomy stalwart of the choral society, the contralto? Musical life is the poorer without her" by Richard Morrison in 'The Times', 28.5.10

AMONGST THE AGED

Some of us improve with age,
Some of us do not
Some rebel and shake their cage,
Some stay mum and rot.
Some, at last, with life engage,
Some sadly lose the plot,
Some will seek another wage,
Some give thanks for what they've got.
Some their lives will judge and gauge,
Some others say it's best forgot.

IN A CORNER OF LINFORD WOOD

They're managing a corner of Linford Wood,
To let in the sun so the wild flowers bud
It always was a damp dark corner,
Stifling its meagre flora and fauna
So to wander in I couldn't resist,
It was something new, not to be missed.
And there it was, completely unexpected,
How long had it been there, undetected?
A pre-Christian rite, at the base of a tree,
A shrine for a boy aged two, maybe three,
The votive offerings were neatly placed
By a family bereft, who in tears embraced
The thought of that family, to their child clutching,
The silence, the sadness; it was all so touching.

BRITS – AN ENDANGERED SPECIES?

My dentist is Ukrainian,
Her assistant Romanian
Our chiropodist is Lithuanian,
And chiropractor Hanoverian
Our waiter is Sicilian,
His colleague Brazilian
The taxi-driver's Hungarian,
The check-out girl Bulgarian
Nail-bar workers are Vietnamese,
The hotel chef is Taiwanese.
The stall-holder's from Afghanistan,
His customers from Uzbekistan
Our library assistant is from Siberia,
The ticket-collector from Liberia
Our next-door neighbour is Jordanian.
The restaurant owner is Iranian.
The postman's Nepalese,
The milkman's Lebanese.

I'm off to join Hans, Pierre and Lazlo in the pub,
To down some Czech Pilsner and some Chinese grub.

LANGUAGE DIFFICULTIES

The German and French that you all sing so lustily
Is out of my reach as my brain grinds but rustily
So I sink in despair; I shouldn't, I know, but I do,
I haven't the flair like you.

But when Britannia sails onto the stage like a stately galleon,
Who then will recall my halting, abysmal grasp of Italian?
As she hoists her colours, waves her flag and sings 'Jerusalem',
I will fill my lungs and sing louder, and show some British phlegm.

July '08 - (During rehearsals for Proms in the Park)

CECIL AND CLAUDE

Whatever happened to humble?
And that stoic expression, "Mustn't grumble"?
To manners, respect and civil pride?
They've disappeared, they've gone out with the tide
To drown in a sea of self-assertion,
Sunk without trace, total immersion
But not quite total, for I heard yesterday
Two old boys to each other say,
An old-time politeness I had to applaud:
"After you Cecil." "No, after you Claude."

HUGS

Along with prescribed medicinal drugs,
I feel there's a place for meaningful hugs
Not that 'kiss of betrayal' the peck on the cheek,
Like a brush of a feather, unbearably weak,
But a full-blooded hug – a human sharing,
A confirmation that someone is caring.
Some say that hugs are no longer PC,
They're unhealthy, a threat or a desperate plea
They are not endangered but they do need a plug,
So please do some healing and indulge in a hug.

ENTHUSIASM PLEASE!

You were always, well, so enthusiastic
Now it's as if you are made of plastic
Over many events you once enthused,
Now it's as if you've been excused.
It's to be expected, the experts tell us,
That the ageing process makes us less zealous,
But that's an unacceptable attitude,
A condescending crappy platitude
It's an opinion that we should with vigour attack
And have it removed like dental plaque.
So get furious, angry, rant and rage,
Show them that passion doesn't die with age
You'll know that something has lit your fuse,
It'll be something over which to enthuse.

INTERNAL REASSURANCE

Karl Marx and Emile Durkheim
Held that we would reach perfection
But I feel we're running out of time
And heading in the wrong direction
That we're looking at a lake of lime,
And badly need a course correction.

Enough! This is too depressing,
Marx and Durkheim may have been right
So stop your grim and gloomy guessing,
True, their aim is not in sight
But even so, we are progressing,
Our long-term future will be bright.

FENELLA FUDGE

She reads the news on Radio 2,
Which is now my station of choice
And I have to admit, between me and you,
That I'm won by the warmth in her voice
Her flawless delivery and impeccable timing,
Combine to set my blood pressure climbing,
Oh Fenella, Fenella, may God be my judge,
I have fallen in love with Fenella Fudge.

(I haven't asked Fenella's permission to include this – but here goes!)

THE FAMILY TREE

"You must come and see the family tree.
It's big and fine – from an ancient line."
"Yes please," I reply, and stifle a sigh,
Because mine of course is like spindly gorse.

It was in the hall and covered a wall,
Selwyns and Dilwyns, Rhys, Prys and Heulwens.
It's shown with a pride, whilst inside I hide
My thin shaky line, my vulnerable vine.

But no need for shame, it's only a game
So then I thought, well, it's high time to tell
Of a gem I can flush from my family bush.
It's time to be proud and shout it out loud:

"My grandfather Dick for a wife did pick,
It's just uncanny, grandmother Fanny."
It's true!

FRIENDS

We have never told our old friends, so they'll never know
How important they were to the ebb and flow of our lives
It's possible that we didn't quite know ourselves
Until this late stage of our journey.

For a while we travelled together, carried along on the same tide
Then we caught different tides, and time and distance
Combined to dilute the relationship
To scribbled notes on Christmas cards.

But they still surface, in conversations,
Or unexpectedly in thoughts, even dreams
Visiting us from what now seems another planet,
But they're there, in the ether and our minds.

So with this knowledge, will we tell our new friends
Just how important they are to us?
Or will we shy away from the opportunity?
Will we be frightfully British about it and leave it unsaid?
Until they too become scribbled notes on Christmas cards,
That will remain, in our stupor, unread.

CONSEQUENCES

Our every act has a consequence, a definite effect,
It's a truth upon which we should pause, and seriously reflect
The word "implies a relationship to what has gone before"*
Even doing nothing, can possibly lead to war,
That every act has a 'knock-on' effect, is a universal fact,
As they're often unintended, we should think before we act
For all our negative consequences, how do we then atone?
It's a problem we all face, and we face it on our own.

*RD Universal Dictionary (1994)

HANS LITTEN (1903-1938)*

Opinions – we're meant to have them,
If we have none we're deemed, judged, to be slow
(Judgement and opinion are first cousins).
But how do we form our opinions
With so little accurate information
Or knowledge upon which to base them?
Do they stem from innate feelings of right and wrong?
But what is right to one generation is wrong to another,
Or are we simply, "Dedicated followers of fashion"?
Are they manufactured by parents, peers and press,
Forged, hammered on an anvil, to produce that monster, public opinion?
Who has the courage to stand in the path of such a tide?
Stand up please Hans Litten, a rock in the face of a monstrous surge,
Until smashed.

In 1931 Hans Litten subpoenaed Hitler to appear in the trial of two SA men accused of murder. Hitler was subjected to a two-hour cross-examination by Litten, an experience Hitler never forgot. On the night of the Reichstag fire, in 1933, Litten was arrested and spent the next five years being tortured in various prisons and camps. Finally, in Dachau, in 1938, he killed himself.

THE MUGGER

I'd run him through with a rusty pitchfork,
That low-life scum who mugged our Kirsty
Yes, I know, of course, this is anger-rich talk,
But just right now I'm, well, bloodthirsty
He needs pulling through with a rag man's trumpet,
Keel hauled and left to lump it,
Yet he's someone's son, and I wonder do they know,
That their once beloved cherub has sunk so low

HYMN NUMBER 193 (A&M REVISED)

In chapel, as lads, we would sing this hymn
With an unrestrained passion, impossible to dim
We were out of tune and in the wrong key,
And we'd grin and snigger with child-like glee
Charles Wesley's words were deemed as divine,
But the attraction to us was the second line,
A line that has sadly remained unforgettable,
And any offence is of course, regrettable.
But only one meaning could we apply,
To "Let me to thy bosom fly".

NO SEX PLEASE, WE'RE BRITISH'

An elegant, elderly lady, just fizzing with effervescence,
Brought to our tutorial group a regal sense of presence
Our oral history tutor had read her autobiography,
Set in colonial East Africa, in the early days of photography.
To his comment, "But your sexual awakening your story skips",
She haughtily replied, with more than a hint of an upper-class sniff,
"My dear boy, the only things that we ever kept stiff
Were our frightfully British upper lips."

Heard during an ice-breaking session on an oral history course during the 1990s.

EDDIE THOMPSON

I CANNOT DO THE RUMBA

Fast approaching sixty-nine, that most suggestive number,
I'm asked to name my deepest shame – I cannot do the rumba.

Leading for me is the problem, communicating by touch,
To be always guided by others, is my psychological crutch.

My failure to dance the rumba is a massive social loss
Why didn't I learn when young, and dance to Edmundo Ros?

The social foxtrot's a breeze, with its quarter turn and chassé
Enid and I together, we feel we look quite classy.

To the gliding steps of the waltz we're gradually warming,
But it's only done as the very last dance, at two o'clock in the morning.

The theory of the quickstep is perfectly clear in my mind,
But the practice, for my partner, is a painful toe-crunching grind.

How sad that I stay at the bar for that Latin American number
When even men with wooden legs get up and do the rumba.

SOMETHING TO TRY AT HOME?

It was May nineteen sixty-two,
And sexual freedom had steamed into view
This can be seen by what had been billed
For the monthly meeting of the Townswomen's Guild
The Kama Sutra, with explanations,
And for added clarity, demonstrations.

Decorum dictates that I say no more,
Besides, they may have breached the law,
Before you ask, in anticipation,
There was no audience participation
It was tastefully done, with couples well skilled,
It was after all, the Townswomen's Guild.

CONTINUITY?

We're raping the earth for resources,
She's under a violent attack
But marshalling her natural forces,
Mother Earth has begun to fight back.

Gaia, of course, will prevail,
To her, over time, be the glory,
Humans, prepare to bewail,
And face the end of our story.

We've confused need with greed,
And the well has ran dry,
We have scattered our seed,
And the end is nigh.
In the space ship 'Noah's Ark'

The chosen few may escape
To set sail in the universe dark
For another planet to rape.

THE NEW REGIME

Please, I implore you, don't think I'm pathetic,
But I'm about to abandon activities athletic
Without a doubt,
Gardening is out
Along with all things rigorous
(Including Tai Chi, far too vigorous).
The off-licence will be the sum of my walks,
The peak of my exercise removing corks
Fruit and veg won't pass my lips,
Instead I'll gorge on fish and chips.
A couch potato is what I'll be
Propped up on cushions, watching TV.
I have three hopes, to live as long as the keep-fit crowd,
With body intact and spirit unbowed.

THANKS BUT NO THANKS

The very word creates a frown,
It is unusual, is it a noun?
"Exfoliation"
Maybe akin to deforestation
We've been asked to enjoy it in the hotel's spa,
We've declined the offer and remain in the bar.
What does it gain us,
A hair-free anus?
Apparently, for the middle classes, it's the latest credential
For the upwardly mobile, the latest essential

A hair-free torso is the ultimate aim,
Body-hair is the ultimate shame.
Well, nobody waxes my waste area,
In beauty treatments, they don't come scarier.

TO THE CHILDREN OF UGANDA

I 'see' you smiling,
Teeth bright white, dazzling, shining
You all look lovely,
Like freshly-drawn water, clean, clear and sometimes bubbly.
What joys you must be,
Well that's how it looks to an old man like me
You are all so rich, and that may strike you as funny,
How can I define your fortune, when it doesn't lie in money?

It's like...
Like...

Like the love that laps around you,
And the wildlife that surrounds you
Like the sun and stars above you,
And your family, who love you
Like clean water, bringing pleasure to you,
And friends that are a treasure to you
Like the hills and the valleys, that are so near and dear to you
And the loss of just one tree, that will bring a mournful tear to you.

This is where your fortune lies,
In your soil, and your roots, and in my envious eyes.

November 2015

LARKRISE VILLAGE TO CANDLEFORD TOWN

Great viewing! Larkrise village to Candleford town,
With the lovely Laura and Thomas Brown
Sunday evenings won't be the same
Without Minnie, Margaret and Dorcas Lane,
And the Timmins's, both Mrs and Mr,
And Sidney, Alfie, Queenie and Twister
The sisters Pratt, with their Paris fashions,
All buttons and bows and bottled up passions.
It's a true portrayal of rural life,
In Victorian times, with poverty rife
Its authenticity can't be contested,
Except, well, those women, they're incredibly high-breasted.

A FOOTBALL FAN'S WISH LIST

May the 'Albions' and 'Athletics' have their time in the sun,
And may Accrington Stanley enjoy a good cup run
To the Football League these clubs bring spice,
And deserve a winning throw of the dice.
So may Plymouth Argyle,
Win the cup in style,
And may Northampton Town
Avoid going down
May the pie stalls never run out of pies,
And may referees have extra eyes
May the spoils of the game be evenly spread,
To help struggling clubs keep out of the red
And when fans drop off this mortal coil, instead of Pearly Gates
Find an electronic turnstile, and on the other side, their mates.

LET'S HEAR IT FOR ANCHORITES

Oh to live in isolation in a disused railway station,
On some ghostly mountain line in a ghastly foreign clime
To neither wash nor shave and to have a foul aroma,
That recognition feature of the dedicated loner.

It's my solitary ambition and it's right for my condition,
There to siphon all my thoughts, with their large and ugly warts
Into a cracked and rusty bucket, smelling faintly of old poo
That was once on platform one, in a gloomy ladies' loo.

To be a crabby hermit, to exist without a permit,

To wave a rude farewell and seek the monk's bare cell

The cold monastic cave, that's the place for me

With the existential question, "To be or not to be?"

A permanent outsider, to life's convoy an outrider,

Socially inept no more, "Gone at last, that frightful bore"

To cast off from the world, from its rotten crumbling jetty,

And to be on nodding terms with a passing upland yeti.

EDDIE THOMPSON

LITTER PICKERS WANTED

We're recruiting litter pickers, with a head for heights
But you must not be averse to cosmic long-haul flights
We're an international company, Orbiting Debris Collectors,
Forming teams of dedicated inner-space protectors
You'll be based on an orbiting satellite litter-station,
In a strange environment of weak gravitation
Competitive rates of pay and a uniform provided
With an umbilical cord, by means of which you're guided
There's a subsidised canteen, offering heavenly views
Where you can mix with tourists on their Virgin Galactic cruise
It's the pinnacle of litter picking,
Apply now, the clock is ticking
You'll have a job with wide horizons, reaching for the stars
This year Milton Keynes, next year maybe Mars.

After reading 'Junk in Space' in 'Eureka', June 2010

RHYTHM

Think of music as religion, with Rhythm as its god,
On giving it some thought, it doesn't sound so odd
"If it ain't got Rhythm, then it don't mean a thing"
Is a line from a song that we, when young, would sing,
Rhythm is omnipotent, it's in a beating heart,
From life as we know it, it can't be prised apart
Everything has Rhythm, seasons, tides, speech, rhyme,
Its 'son' is mathematics, this we see in time
So, all hail Rhythm, hosannas to our head,
And let us all acknowledge that without it, we'd be dead.

LOSERS

Stroke them and they purr,
So, to what do I refer?
God's gift to creation,
Or at very least the nation,
Antagonistic,
Apt to go ballistic
Corrosive, coercive,
Competitive, furtive
Testosterone fired,
For bragging hard-wired
Conversations of instructions
And fantasy seductions
Egos overblown,
As 'me me me' they drone.
You may feel from this description
This is not a work of fiction,
There are of course exceptions, let's not be too cruel
But we all know exceptions simply prove the rule
On reaching line ten you'd have recognized then,
The sad losers I refer to are of course men.

THE OPTIMISM OF THE FOOTBALL FAN

The football season starts today
Of course it will bring both joy and dismay
Our hopes and expectations are high,
But dreams of success may be pie in the sky.
Come April we may wonder why
Success so cruelly passed us by
We'll fail to see either rhyme or reason,
But we know it will come for sure next season.

EDDIE THOMPSON

O'DONOVAN'S OBOE

On the Victory Parade of '46,
As the tanks rolled by King George the Sixth,
All was not as it seemed
For a gay young commander,
With commendable candour,
Stood erect in his turret and beamed.

Between you and me
What the King couldn't see
Was a breach of his own Regulations
The commander's wide smile,
(An unmilitary style)
Caused many to voice speculations.

Though some were verbose,
No guess could come close
To the ongoing illegal no-no
For the officer was pleasured
By his gunner (whom he treasured),
Who was playing on his personal pink oboe.★

★*A phrase used by comedian Peter Cooke in a satirical sketch about the Jeremy Thorpe trial*

ON NOT BEING BUSY

Because we're becalmed, we're led to believe
That we don't belong; we're beaten, berated,
Belittled, bemused
But this beggars belief,
Bemeaned be damned!
Be still, we beseech you
Be done with this bequest
Besides, we're not beyond, we're in between
Be warned, beware, we're about to begin.
On realising that doing nothing is OK.

OSCAR

For colourful characters, the Lancers never lacked
With charismatic characters the Regiment was packed
But one, a lovable rogue, stands out amongst them all
In Regimental folk-lore, Oscar Harmon's standing tall
And Oscar's death last week
Has driven home the fact that Oscar was unique
By the Brigadier and Colonel, 'Oscar' he was known,
So infamous and widespread had his reputation grown
When old comrades gather and the pot of memories stirred
Bubbling up to the surface, tales of Oscar will be heard
These are tales of the unexpected,
Of crimes against the Army Act, mostly undetected.
So who will write the book, who will make a start?
Who will make the film, who could play his part?

It has been arranged that he'll be met at the Pearly Gates,
By a welcoming party of his old army mates.

FLUID RECALL

It's blacker than the blackest night,
Topped by an inch of off-white white
And in the glass, in the smell and the taste,
There's a time remembered, a youth retraced,
Of Saturday nights with the boys, long gone,
The Bridge, the Britannia, the Saddle, the Swan
It's more than a drink, it's a personal tradition,
It's also a medicine for whatever my condition
So in the good times and the bad, I will never be without
A bottle, or a glass, of my saviour: Irish stout.

PROPER POETRY

Last night
I heard proper poetry
performed with such a passion
that I now know
my silly little six-liners
should be shredded for compost.

so i'm doing away with capital letters
and commas at the end of each line
if they think that's too unconventional
or controversial that's fine
rhyming couplets will have to go too
and i'll pluck up the courage my soul to bare
i'll be radical, loud, crude and swear
i want to be different like you
but hang about, i'm feeling uneasy

light-headed, uncomfortable, slightly queasy
i suppose i prefer order and structure
lines that rhyme, not chaos and rupture
in this undisciplined unfettered anarchy
i feel lost, exiled, alien and panicky
Maybe i'll stay in my comfort zone
I feel better already.

After attending a 'Tongue in Chic' poetry meeting in Mencap Theatre, Wolverton, Milton Keynes. March 2009

ROBERTA OF NASH

She's six feet five and she slinks on the stage
With a figure resembling a tyre pressure gauge
She sports pale woollen socks and facial hair
And she glides 'round the band in the spotlight's glare.

The crowd go wild as she wiggles her hips
And men at the front choke on their chips
She's hinged in the middle and sways to the beat
And taps out the rhythm with her size twelve feet.

With a red plastic bag tucked under her arm,
She's an image drawn from the fantasy farm
The drummer, the singer, in fact all the band,
Are fondled in turn by the nymph's free hand.

She exits stage left and waves a goodbye,
Then cheekily gives us a flash of her thigh.
Who is she? Who cuts such a sensuous dash?
It isn't, it is, Roberta of Nash.

- October 2001

To commemorate Robert Meardon's appearance on stage, in drag, during an MK Chorale's local talent night.

ROSIE AND NOEL'S 60TH

They're sixty, and overflowing with life
I refer to Noel, and Rosie, his wife,
In their ever-welcome presence
You can't miss their effervescence
Soon, before I'm too far gone,
I hope to find out what they're on!
They're warm and comforting, like a well-worn glove
Of course! That's it – it's the power of love.

URBAN STUDIES

Today we'll discuss urban sprawl
Does it appeal or does it appal?
Followed by urban depredation,
And inner-city deprivation.
After lunch it's urban decay,
And its associated violent, noisy affray.

Tomorrow, a seminar on urban congestion,
After which we're open to suggestion
Perhaps a debate on urban squalor,
Chaired by a well-known urban scholar
Who then, to avoid complete consternation,
Will wind things up with gentrification.

SO WHAT DO I BELIEVE?

Where do I stand on, say, reincarnation?
Or, now that I've mentioned it, expiation?

And there's that old chestnut predestination
And what about transubstantiation?

Should I follow fundamentalists,
Or maybe egg on existentialists?

The menu is long and far from informing,
To all free thinkers it acts as a warning.

Sociobiologists, evangelicals,
Pantheists, atheists, ecumenicals

Conspiracy theorists, eschatology,
The feeling that Judas may be owed an apology.

I can't be doing with things theological,
They sound as sane as things mythological.

Virgin birth, original sin I just can't understand
And cults led by charlatans, all underhand.

Mother Earth, shamanism, ancient cosmology,
Good Fortune, Druidism, Scientology

Terry Pratchett, Dan Brown, Marian adoration,
And who are the chosen ones, guaranteed salvation?

So then, what do I believe? Well, I've decided
I believe that we are all mysteriously guided.

SOCIAL TRENDS?

Egos now are over-inflated,
Humility is way outdated
Honesty is zero-rated,
And to deviousness we're inculcated.

We've succumbed to the seduction
Of conspicuous consumption,
But the seeds of our destruction
Lie in the ubiquitous corruption.

We're being groomed to compete
And not to consider defeat,
For the winner has garlands laid at his feet
All hail the immoral, universal cheat.

A FLASH IN THE PARK

Walking her dogs around Tongwell Lake,
Friend Helen, shocked, did a double take,
For there before her, on a steep grassy bank,
Stood a DIY fan, enjoying, al fresco, a J. Arthur Rank.
Helen ran, with an Olympic pace,
But with his trousers down, there wasn't a chase
That he would have caught her is extremely doubtful,
And friend Liz declared, she'd have given him a mouthful. (?)

STEREOTYPING

Stereotyping makes us lazy,
It renders our thoughts somewhat hazy
It keeps them in a mode close to sleep,
And we apply the stereotype in one broad sweep.
For example, academics are all absent minded,
By the stereotype we're blinkered, some would say blinded
Or, the English are stiff upper lipped and reserved,
To those who know better, that's blatantly absurd.
The Scots fight, the Welsh sing, the Irish drink,
Explanations are simple, we don't have to think
So there we have it, attractive to non-thinkers,
Stereotyping, or putting on blinkers.

THE QUAVER

A quaver,
The whole quaver – to hold and savour.
The semi-quaver,
Half the whole but retaining its flavour.
The demi-semi quaver,
Small and perfectly formed – a right little raver.
The hemi-demi-semi-quaver,
The blink of an eye – the infinitesimal time-saver.

EDDIE THOMPSON

THE MATCH

How was the match, dear? Don't ask, we lost,
It's the coldest night of the year dear,
Me eyebrows were coated with frost.

There were no programmes, the editor's ill,
The kick-off was late, their driver got lost,
Me pie was cold, me feet are still.

We had two sent off and five yellow cards,
We missed a penalty; it sailed over the bar,
And their only goal was offside by yards.

I missed your flask of soup, and your pickle sandwich
If I'd any sense I'd have stayed in the car,
The manager was banned for using foul language.

Their keeper was carried off on a door,
They couldn't find the stretcher
Even then we couldn't score.

Twice we hit the upright,
And the lights went out for a quarter of an hour
It was then that the crowd got uptight.

Well, there wasn't much of a crowd, really, very few,
The sensible ones remained in the bar
On the touch-line I counted just twenty-two.

So you'll give it a miss on Saturday dear?
What! Come Hell or high water, hail rain or shine,
I'll be there, my beloved, on the touchline.

THE MATING GAME

What utter fools we are, we men
(To think it's a game where we set the rules
I'll say it again – what utter fools.)

How easily beguiled we are,
(By those enticingly baited honey-traps,
What perfectly ridiculous saps.)

A glance, a smile and we're totally hooked,
(Feminine charms and a raised hem
Make putty of the strongest men.)

How easily we swallow the bait,
(How subtle, how sleek,
How pathetically weak.)

How our egos are pampered
(It's me, I'm the fellow,
How tragically shallow.)

How we think we're in charge,
(We're buffoons with loud voices,
Who just can't see that they make the choices.)

Of course, it will ever be the same,
(Otherwise the species stalls,
That's why our brains are in our smalls.)

HE CAN DO BETTER

Time flies by
Like the blink of an eye,
Our three score and ten
Will be over, what then?
Recycled? It's just a thought,
A sentence from an on-high court
Sent back with fresh beginnings,
Sent in for a second innings.
The purpose will be to get off our laurels,
To change our behaviour, improve our morals
We'll have two more tries to turn it about,
As it says in the Bible, three strikes and you're out.

TOMMY THE TUP'S LAST STAND

Tommy the Tup died in an ithyphallic state
His Marquis of Lorne was enormous, due to his diet of skate
This presented a problem, for the lid we couldn't close,
So after a brief debate, this cunning plan we chose
(We were putting him in his coffin, this I should have made clear
And I was a young apprentice, green behind the ear.)
We chalked around his todger, on the lid, on the underside,
When one of the joiners in envy and growing wonder cried,
"This should be in a museum, pickled and placed on display,
For all men to behold, and admire in awe and dismay".
So we cut a neat hole in the lid and passed his Percy through,
And guided by the foreman, we knew exactly what to do.
Flush with the lid, his John Thomas we cut,
Then sanded it down when the lid was screwed shut.
It was varnished and polished as if on a yacht,
And when finally finished, it looked just like a knot.

THE SOLOIST

She stood so proud and sang so loud,
Every note she would master.
That English rose with perfect pose,
And breasts of alabaster.*
On curtain calls in concert halls
From Kent to old Lancaster,
When bowing low they stole the show,
Those breasts of alabaster.
They're held in place by frilly lace,
And maybe sticking plaster
I can't recall her voice at all,
Just breasts of alabaster.

*a phrase borrowed from the
Jake Thackray song 'It Was Only a Gypsy'

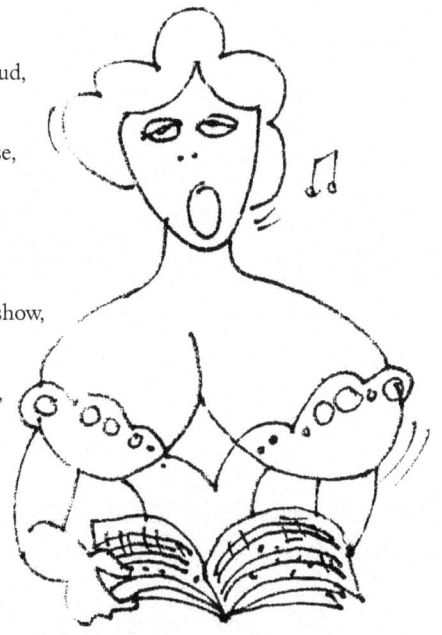

TO MK'S CRITICS

Wave upon wave of criticism
Is thrown at Milton Keynes,
An incessant stream of cynicism
Is served by the media's queens.
But let them all pontificate,
Let them huff and puff,
Let them joke and deprecate,
We don't give a stuff.

EDDIE THOMPSON

ONE FOR THE CHILDREN

Our Manx cat Orry
Isn't all there,
If that sounds cruel I'm sorry,
And I ask you not to stare.
The part that's missing is his tail,
He has instead a stump
You've noticed? You can hardly fail,
Some have less - a rump.
It's Mother Nature's blunder,
And it looks a little rum
I sometimes – often – wonder,
Is he cold around the bum?

WE'LL MEET AGAIN...

Q: A rock the size of the moon is speeding towards us through space
So here's the question. How do we save the human race?
We've got until Friday to come up with a wheeze,
So answers on a postcard please.

A: there's no point, we keep calm and carry on,
At the time of impact, around a quarter to ten,
We all join hands and sing this song:
"We'll meet again, don't know where don't know when..."

HARMONY

To be in harmony with others,
that's what singing's about,

To lift your voice in song is
akin to the primeval shout

It's a pressure release valve,
relieving stress,

It's therapeutic, a
mental caress.

"Harmony, an agreement
of feeling"

Of its definitions, that's the
most appealing.

That it's all about feelings in my mind
there's no doubt,

To be in harmony with others, that's what singing's about.

WELSH WORDS

Rules dictate

That Welsh words mutate

Learners get over it,

We've just got to go for it.

Yes, it is very strange

That they undergo change,

But it helps the words to roll off the tongue

It gives them a rhythm, as if they were sung.

BERYL AND BERT

We have a pair of pigeons, feral,
We call him Bert, the female Beryl
They seem to live in our back garden,
And if what I say offends, I do beg your pardon,
But Beryl is broody,
Whilst Bert is moody,
And with disgraceful aloofness, he spurns her advances,
And likewise he ignores her meaningful glances,
But Beryl persists,
Whilst Bert resists,
With her billing and cooing,
But Bert is indifferent to her purposeful wooing,
We stand at the door and shout, "Beryl, ignore him!"
But no, she prostates herself before him
This is an offer even he can't refuse,
But his grudging acceptance we will not excuse.
In three seconds flat the deed is done,
Three seconds! Poor Beryl, that can't have been fun.
Then Bert waddles off to lie down in the shade,
And Beryl must wonder, has she been laid?
It would serve him right if he were to discover
That Beryl had flown, with a better lover.

WHO IS THIS GUY BIGGLES?

A few years ago
an American pilot attached to the Royal Air Force
at RAF Valley, Anglesey,
was practising low-level flying
in the valleys of Snowdonia
when he was puzzled by an instruction
painted in large white letters on a farmhouse roof.
His question that night gave the barmaid giggles:
"What does it mean, BUGGER OFF BIGGLES?"

THE CORNER SHOP

I had to stop and stand and stare,
For the sign said clearly, `Fetish Wear'
On the corner shop in Bryony Place
I should keep it in mind, just in case
I'm ever invited to a Fetish Fantasia,
Why are you laughing? I can think of things crazier
I wouldn't want to be the guest
That knocks on the door improperly dressed,
Turning up in a battered sou-wester,
And an army gas-mask, left for years to fester,
Just wouldn't cut the mustard, I'd be disgraced
Who would dress in such shocking bad taste?

I wonder what it is they sell,
And who exactly are their clientele?
All things considered, I very much doubt
That Enid and I are missing out.

LONGER ONES

Yes, it is unusual, and it may not be wise,
It may be too unorthodox
To arrange these verses by size.

For your health's sake sing
I'm H-A-P-P-Y
Listening to the Clock
The RE lesson
Calch Fynydd

FOR YOUR HEALTH'S SAKE, SING

There's a song to suit our every emotion
And the following menu offers up choices
Of times and reasons for raising our voices,
To enable a sip from this feel-good potion.

Marches to sing, for the militaristic
G and S, for the mildly satirical
Raps and chants, for the wildly political
Mantras to hum, for the spiritualistic.

Flamenco, for the seriously wild,
Barbershop, for the obsessively cheerful
Portuguese Fado, to make you tearful
A lullaby, to soothe the child.

When we're depressed, there's always the blues,
For those departed, a requiem mass
Or auditions that you want to pass,
Calypsos, on a West Indian cruise.

National anthems, for the nationalistic,
Sing-along songs, like songs from the shows,
Karaoke, where anything goes,
A chant with a drum, for the shamanistic.

Folk and trad, for the atavistic
Bawdy ballads in a rugby club
Free-range singing in a licensed pub
Chapel hymns, for the Calvinistic.

EDDIE THOMPSON

Witty chants from the gasworks end,
Welsh penillion for serious singing,
Sopranos' descants 'round rafters ringing,
Glee-club sessions, where voices blend.

Shanties, always, to get the job done,
A serenade, to win a lover,
A Sinatra song, from an album cover,
Rounds at a camp fire, for having fun.

There's minimalism, for the futuristic,
Rock 'n' roll or carols, madrigals or pop,
Mouth-music, party-songs, chants from Anfield's Kop
A chorus from Carmen, for the pugilistic.

So face the world squarely, like a professional:
On the notes that you like, let it all out.
If you feel you can't sing, then let out a shout,
It's therapeutic, kind of, like the confessional.

I'M H-A-P-P-Y

It's an odd sort of word isn't it, I mean 'happy'?
Say it slowly and feel the fun, it's a ha-ha word
It seems closely related to dippy and dappy,
Or am I becoming an etymological nerd?

They make you smile, flappers and slappers, happy-clappies
It's something to do with the double 'p',
Puppies and yuppies, crappy nappies,
I'm being flippant, but then, that's me.

Look at Larry, he's always been happy
Slipping happy pills with that happy band
In hippy dress looking vaguely snappy,
Seeking happy thrills in their happy land.

But just for a moment, let's be serious,
Which, if you're happy, is difficult to do
Let's make the word 'happy' mysterious,
And take an academic view.

It isn't easy to recognize the state,
It's elusive and difficult to savour
Invariably it comes to us late,
When it's difficult to recall the flavour.

To look for it is counter-productive
For it lurks in unlikely places,
Whilst material wealth is seductive,
Light is provided by smiling faces.

The best we can hope for is a happy medium
Midway between gleeful and sad,
So long as we miss boring tedium
And peak at a level marked 'glad'.

And when at last our travails cease
And we face the ultimate power,
Will we find that our happy release
Is just one long happy hour?

All together now:
I know I am, I'm sure I am,
I'm H-A-P-P-Y.

LISTENING TO THE CLOCK

Listen, I've never heard our clock tick so loud
It must be the stillness – and my new hearing aid.
It's a modern clock, just twenty years old,
But unusual for a modern clock, it has a slow, and tonight loud, tick.

The point is, it's bringing back childhood memories
Of Sunday visits to Uncle Jim and Aunty Nellie
In the tiny village of Maughold, on the Isle of Man.
They had a grandfather clock with a proper tick, lazy and loud

I can hear it clearly now, above the noise of four children,
Mary, Frances, Jimmy the baby and me, playing on the floor and
Above the conversation of the 'grown-ups' around the inglenook fireplace,
Where the men are drinking ale and everybody laughs at the tall tales.

It was at that fireplace that I had my first taste of beer,
And wondered how on earth they could drink the stuff
The talk must have had a serious side too,
As Uncle Jim and my father would soon be off to war.

But we'd be too engrossed in play to pick that up
(Uncle Jim was my father's uncle really, but of a similar age)
This tick of our modern clock has turned on a 'replay' action
That rekindles sounds, smells and sights that have been long buried.

Like the four-mile ride on the old blue bus (old even then) from Ramsey
To see a table overflowing with food, and timber beams in the ceiling,
The smell of the paraffin lamps and the steep step up into the kitchen.
Years later the hidden corner of this step was found to hold a message in
Ogham script.

I can see us collecting eggs in the barn and running along the cliff tops
It all seems so wholesome, so innocent, so lovely,
I'm walking now, at the end of the visit, in the dark, with my parents,
Sometimes on my father's shoulders

Along the narrow, empty country road to the tram stop at Dreemskerry
Listening at the poles for the last tram to take us back to Ramsey.

I'll just sit here for a while longer, in the stillness,
Listening to the tick of the clock.

THE RE LESSON

"Today we're going to talk about Heaven,"
Said Miss Mavis Davies, the RE teacher
(whose father, 'Save us' Davies, was a Wesleyan preacher).

So Doris Morris, give her her due,
Stood up first to voice her view

(Now Horace Morris, the father of Doris, is the village drunk.)
"Please Miss," said Doris, "My dad wishes that he had the key,
'Cos he reckons up there, the beer is free."

Said Primrose Pritchard,
(Whose sister Cilla was a worthy winner in this year's Urdd Eisteddfod)
"My mam says it's a vast Marks and Spencer's,
With help-yourself- cash dispensers."

Evan Bevan
(Whose father Kevin is a committed communist)
And who once gave Anwen Branwen a very soggy public kiss,
Shocked the class again by saying, "It's a lot of rubbish, Miss".

POETRY FREE RANGE

Said Joanna Jones,
(Whose Dad, Jones the Bones, was once a first-aider down the pit)
As she sucked her thumb and twizzled her hair,
"It must be nice 'cos my puppy-dog's there."

Sali Mali,
(Whose mother Martha is the Mayor of Merthyr)
Stated loudly, "We've nothing to fear about being dead,
'Cos they all speak Welsh in Heaven – Mam said."

Huw Pugh,
(Whose Aunty Sue lives in sin with Gareth Wyn)
Had heard that only tenors get through the gates,
As basses are shackled with heavy weights.

Barry Parry,
(Whose cousin Garry was injured down the mine)
Looked Miss straight in the eye and said, "My Dad says the same as Evan,
It's just a massive con, is Heaven."

Dai Shy,
(Whose Granddad Nye had been a chapel deacon)
Whispered to his chest, "It's full of angels all in white,
Where mams and dads never fight."

Carys Harris,
(Whose uncle has played for Wales, in Paris)
Announced that her idea of Heaven,
Was "Wales forty, England seven."

EDDIE THOMPSON

Hâf Price
(Whose name she bewails, for she's called by the boys, 'Summer Sales')
Asked, "When we're in Heaven, will we still be the same?
Well, d'you think they'll let me change my name?"

Angharad Hopkins-Watkins,
Whose mother once danced with the Prince of Wales –
before, that is, she went off the rails)
Said, "Mummy says that Heaven is floating along on cloud nine,
With magic mushrooms and Buckfast wine."

All thirty-two aired a view,
Then Miss was asked to air hers too,
She was prepared to say, complete understanding, perfect peace,
Where all our toils and conflicts cease,
But on digesting what she had heard,
Thought that that would sound absurd
So she took a deep breath and blurted out
(Well, to be honest, it was more like a shout)
"Dressed to the nines, with Jimmy Choo shoes,
On a dinner date, with a hunk like Tom Cruise."

CALCH FYNYDD

We're living in a place that was once called Calch Fynydd*
In the lee of the Chilterns, South Midlands, not Gwynedd.

Freely translated from Welsh, it refers to a hill of chalk,
Which well describes the landscape when seen from the Ridgeway walk.

Calcified place names remain, to give up hints of its history
Strange clusters of blood groups add to a tantalising mystery

The invading Saxons seemingly disliked the tiniest hill,
So they circumvented the Chilterns, to regroup later by Brill.

The locals, known to learned historians as Celts or Romano-British,
Were called by the Saxons 'Welsh', which was seriously skittish.

This Saxon word means `foreigner', an obvious misnomer,
For the realm belonged to the Celt, clearly the rightful owner.

Saxon encroachment was constant, despite a stubborn resistance
The locals delayed their advance, defending their very existence.

EDDIE THOMPSON

The Chilterns became an oasis, an isle in a sea of strangers,
Facing a death by absorption, they were well aware of the dangers.

Sadly they slowly succumbed to centuries of Saxon attrition,
Both their language and their culture were steadily starved of nutrition.

What now of those people of Avalon, with their apples ever sweet?
What signs of their cultural legacy can be seen in a Wendover street?

Are there Druids still in Dunstable, a bard in Beaconsfield?
Does the Gorsedd meet in secret where once the princes kneeled?

Is there singing still in Risborough, in the heart of our lost lands?
Is there someone wearing woad in the woods by Woburn Sands?

But all is not completely lost, for in eighteen eighty-five,
Scholars** discovered a distinct racial strain, the pedigree is still alive!

*   *Rutherford Davis K (1982) 'Britons and Saxons, The Chiltern Region 400-100', Phillimore.*

** *Beddoe J (1885) 'The races of Britain' passim Fleure (1951) 'A Natural History of Britain' p144 and fig. 43.*

EPILOGUE

You will now be well aware that I haven't gone for quality,
As most of these verses are couched in frivolity
To put them in a genre, would be quite absurd
('genre' is a hoity-toity, wishy-washy word)
And they may be symptoms of a shameful waste of time,
Putting people and places and memories to rhyme,
But they might fit 'Pub Poetry'', which leads me on to think,
That they might scan better if you read them with a drink
But if these poems have generated just one wide smile,
Then the time has not been wasted, it has all been worthwhile.

www.ingramcontent.com/pod-product-compliance
Lightning Source LLC
Chambersburg PA
CBHW061337040426
42444CB00011B/2967